The Perspective Reality

Juan Solares

India | USA | UK

Made with ❤ on the BookLeaf Publishing Platform
www.bookleafpub.in
www.bookleafpub.com

Dedication

You have become my inspiration and motivation to grow into the best version of myself. The limitless and unconditional depths of your love empowers the composing of this vast vernacular.

~Texas Toast~

Preface

Acknowledgements

1. The GUTTERS

Mr. & Mrs. Gutter, a union so odd.
Consumed by only deception and fraud.

A magnificent collaboration of mental health, alcohol,
drug, spousal, and child abuse so profound.
It'd be wise to invest in a monthly subscription dedicated
to therapeutic counseling sessions to freely go around.
I am positive you could cover the wages,
From the income you generate on your CamSoda XXX
pages.

One day you and your husband may be forced to abort
the operation, once the government discovers they have
been providing free handouts towards fraudulent
desperation.

At which point you would end up in court, with a lawyer
that performs pro bono work.
This would be your allowance to perform another pro
bono jerk.

It'd quench your uncanny thirst for any man's
validation.
Thus, leading to a pearl necklace of your favorite

libation.
As you engulfed every inch with no hesitation.
And, these are the behaviors you exhibit globally, and
across the U.S. Nation?

If the community only knew the truth you'd be a
disgrace.
But, your marriage remains shameless and in place,
Because you both rejoice when receiving cream pies to
the face.

The only constant is manipulation and lies.
A disgusting revelation humanity witnesses within their
eyes.
You two are Scooby Doo, but monsters in human
disguise.
Vile evil creatures, who next to shit would collect
majority of the flies.
And, find a nesting home to procreate life in between
both of your thighs.
What you hold dear is the riddles of STI's.

Two peas bound together, in a rotting and decaying pod.
I await with happiness, to place my gaze upon you lying
under eternal sod.

We concealed your truth to prevent the humiliation of

your exposure.
However, the time has arrived for your full sinful
disclosure.

Funny how your marriage was not there to be exposed,
yet you would have sex to sell your pantyhose.
Amazon or EBay, anything for profit.
The highest bidder would earn a pornographic view,
possibly even two, not even the lack of your morals or
values maintained the ability to stop it.

Defiling your soul for any form of validation or
monetary gain.
Yet, the Gutter family had the audacity to slander my
name?

Your toxic past consumed with shame, and all the
behaviors you have been trained to display.
A legal form of prostitution is closed claim to fame, and
how your family got paid.
Sorry, not sorry it had to go this way.
Your unions indecency on the internet will eternally
remain.

Truth is I cannot stomach either face.
You are blessed I have not chosen for you two unfit
parents to catch another DHHS case.

Child Protective Services at a snap could be at your
place.
My only prevention is having your children relocated
into a system of disgrace.

I have witnessed the neglect and abuse you present your
children as if it was a gift.
Leaving a three year old alone in a vehicle for prolonged
periods of time.
An older son you'd strike in the back of the head with
extreme force, deemed you as Motherly slime.
A highly sexualized daughter whose behavior you
promote and endorse.
For all your shortcomings, it would be life I encourage
you both to divorce.

With these words I am sincerely being soft.
Without you two scumbags your children would
seriously be better off.

As a Father, don't bother.
As a Mama, you are the living epitome of parental
trauma.
As parental units combined you are the deliverance of
the Adverse Child Experience.

Understand clearly, I would never offer either of you a

resolution.
This is my declaration of your eradication by
persecution, or any common interest solution.
Kindness towards either of you I will never fall slave, yet
the euphoric gate of heaven would open for me once I
pissed on your graves.

This is the collision of my ethers disposition.
This type of sensation allows my soul to burn slow.
No existence of submission defines every calculated
decision.
To be executed with efficiency and immaculate precision.

The mixture of anger and passion forge revenge.
I will not consume hate while you continue to survive.
I have declared it is peace I am willing to give.
An olive branch that permits both of you to live.

Please do not take my kindness for weakness, and allow
my words to be absorbed.
And do not forget I possess the power to strike you two
snakes down, with my sword, if I get bored.

This is no threat by any means.
This is how you two would enter eternal dreams.

2. The MUSICAL BICYCLE

Musically you march to the beat of your own
dysfunctional drum.
While polish all instruments with saliva and cum.
Even thinking your name makes me feel dumb.
How did I ever involve myself with such a piece of scum.

You cheated on your husband,
I should have been wiser.
Claiming to be victim.
It was your narcissistic ways.
Every teacher became enlightened to your whorish
plays.

Educators see clearly through how truly transparent you
are.
Off of mere talent you will not make it far.
Better keep exercising your slutty sexual par.
The only thing you have to offer is a chocolate star.

The class you present respectfully degrades the entire
female gender.
You are the masterful,
ultimate innocence pretender.

Your tears would flood a box of tissues.
Due to your choices and self-inflicted mentally unstable
issues.

Anna once lies with the powers of a black smith.
However, you are deserving of the darkness that comes a
long with the Reapers black kiss.

Your nickname developed for being a popular ride.
Now you are rotting internally from the hundreds of
men's semen swimming inside.

I truly hope you read this and your soul gets shook.
My only request is you burn as you cook,
and please don't forget the Hue of Blu book.

You said it yourself, you're not a good person.
I hope you enjoyed your malicious fun,
because karma is real with all the evil you have done.

Your musical talent is what you are determined to pass.
Unfortunately, the only talent you possess is giving away
free donations of your ass.

3. Dark to Light

My mind races faster than the speed of light
Not fully understanding how to conquer this fright
Positive vibration I'll continue to seek
Util my life has reached its final peak
I speak of times and emotions familiar to many
This evil has no rival and has an army of many
But I will not surrender to this dangerous manifestation
of my own imagination
I've made the choice to strike back with no hesitation
nor lack of motivation
I will be victorious no matter the situation
The positive power of love is the ultimate weapon
People try to use evil, yet have a total misconception
Not fully understanding their direction
The energy we take is like eating a meal
Do that for a while and see how you truly feel
We are all faced with the same struggle of literally living
in division
Anxiousness takes ahold of the steering wheel of life
That cuts through our souls like ice
My loves clear vision with targeting precision
Keeping my order and structure to not seem mad
Unfortunately, the energetic line passing through me is
eternal grief for all of humanity

It is undeniable how this saddens defines my existence
within this realm
Yet, humanity becoming untied can prevail over this
temporary inferno of hell
Compassion and love should be the only contagions at
this stage in life
Love so strong it allows the blind to obtain sight
The ingredient so powerful it allows the weak to have
might
Without prejudice or doubt, and regardless of emotional
definition
The type of force that knows no submission, yet beware
of the collision
I will stand over my loved ones as a watcher and protect
to never allow any evil to invade our sector
Living positively is life truest undeniable nectar
So, I'll keep my faith in my universal protector
The world must recognize we are sisters and brothers
sharing the same pain
Attempts to rationalize this all in your brain maintains
the ability to drive you insane
Operating on a higher frequencies is difficult to obtain
Yet, the stars are placed in your hands for you to
rearrange
Some call it the Bible and some call it one of life's
negative cycle
I dubbed it an enlightened awakening and natural arrival

of human survival
This Earth for the moment is where we belong
So, please stay united to remain mentally, emotionally,
and physically strong

4. Toxic Marvels of Transformation

We dispute over a meaning I hold so deep.
You follow blindly your own imagined sheep.
Your mentally deterioration due to lack of sleep.
It is possible this union has reached its peak.
A glimpse into the future I wish we could sneak.
Anxiety so crippling it strengthens us to be weak.
Shining seconds is what we seek.
Days so glorious it allows a mute to speak.
Waters so treacherous they transform to smooth and sleek.

5. Love At My Feet

I sprint from adversity to you.

Your beauty is breathtaking.

The creativity you inspire makes me marvel.

You are the union to cultural divide.

Anyone who loves you speaks a universal language.

Your captivation motivates wars to stop.

For you, I permit my blood, sweat, and tears to flow freely.

To you, endless energy is donated until I sleep.

Merely the thought of you gifts me butterflies in my stomach.

A ball is all that is needed to reach my individual peak.

For you futbol, there is love at my feet.

6. It Once Was

We found each other in a time of despair.
I recall falling in love with your gaze, your stare.
How I longed for the scent of your hair.
You made me believe it was until the end of time.
I was too deep in the woods, so my love was blind.
The greatest gift you gave took nine months in the
making.
Without warning you made the decision it was yours for
the taking.
It was clearly witnessed through the fog it was love you
were faking.
At the cost of me and our child you began your evil
twisted plays.
The apple did not fall far from the tree with your
narcissistic ways.
You seek any form of social media validation introducing
your smear campaigns.
Never an idea or second thought about what our
daughter may grow to hear.
Now I leave it to karma, so it is life you should fear.
I loved you enough to release the steering wheel.
Now I see truth, and do not speak or feel.
The creation of my identity minus you gifts me altitude,
with a peaceful buzz.

The depths of my soul breeds freedom and joy because, it once was.

7. My First

Gorgeous, Glamorous
Intelligent, Insightful
Scintillating, Sarcastic
Eloquent, Ecstatic
Luminous, Lovely
Lavish, Luxurious
Elegant, Empowered

8. My Second

Magical, Marvelous, Magnificent
Adorable, Adventurous, Awesome
Valuable, Visionary, Victorious
Elegant, Excellence, Ebullient
Nurturing, Noble, Nice

9. The Sewage Symphony

Walking sewage between your thighs.
Everyone laughs at your crossed eyes.
People gaze upon your facade with despise.
Ha. Ha. Ha. More crocodile cries.
Your adultery is why your marriage is dead.
Musically twisted, psychotic head.
You'd welcome ANY warm body into your bed.
A simple blink motivates your legs to spread.
Your promiscuous addiction will soon have you STI dead.
Due to sexually disgusting and corrosive needs you are
not blessed with seeds.
Thus, cursed with a vaginal canal that eternally bleeds.
You're a TINDER right of pASSage.
And, communal usage.
Everyone witnessed you trying to be slick.
I wouldn't recommend touching you with my worst
enemies dick.

10. Welcome to the Circus

Once upon a time
I ate glue and slime
I must confess
When I was six years old, I wore a dress
Fast forward 30 years
I'm still a man child in tears
Allow me to alleviate your fears
Only after a six pack of beer
In a land full of ice and snow
I still preferred Columbian blow
I can't multitask
Because I live in a cerebral cast
But there's still time
To get with the rhythm and rhyme
So I close my eyes and beat my meat
Until I levitate up off my feet
Until the end I will stand true
I'll always love Winnie the Pooh
Nothing more, nothing less
It's your titties I wanna caress.

Sharon Dix & Cox

11. April Fool's

I came in hard, like a hurricane
I feel soulless, Novocain
Your weakness I will consume
My orgasmic pleasure you will swallow down to your
womb
Driving thoughts, maddening desire
Which leads to your crotch being on fire
Mechanical motions, a riot starts
Irritable bowel syndrome, rancid farts
Castaway dreams, thoughtless pillows
Sun kissed skin and blown away willows
A melody of lies whispers within
Living life fully leads to joyful sin
I'd cross oceans to melt your eyes
If you were vanilla ice cream, I'd use you to dip my fries
With no arms and bionic legs
I'd look like a TRex with mini pegs
Feel the thunder, hear my pain
See my noise, taste my rain
Fuck this mess, I'm out
I'm like a teapot short and stout

Sharon Dix & Cox

12. The Romantic Coin

The Romantic Coin

My soul lingers for your scent
Forbidden love, leaving just a hint
Your lips gift passionate quivers
Kisses down my spine sends shivers
Our energies latch to never part
In your fingers, there lies my heart
My love would move mountains and drink the sea
An eternal fire consumes you and me
For Pandoras Box you are the key
A shadowy night, silky breeze
Disguised in sacrifice is my pleasure
My hearts secret treasure
Your name echoes with repetitive bliss
Never in a million years would I replace this
Our auras intertwine with magnificent leisure
I burn for you, a 3 am fever
Continuous lust like a one night stand
Inhaling you, like contraband
Without you, I would love nevermore
Instead I'll spend my life with you, forevermore.

Sharon Dix & Cox

13. Order of Operation

Beautiful sun ray.
Thunderous storm.
Laboring donkey.
Mystical unicorn.

Degenerate sinner.
Holy saint.
Perfection.
Mistake.

The real.
The fake
Gift of life.
Last breath you take.

14. Mind Power

Whirlwind of thoughts.
Energy of transformation.
Words become scripture.
Good or evil.
We paint the picture.
Rippling power of choice.
Affect unknown.
Manifested change.
Effect acknowledged.
Positive or negative.
Perspective reality.

15. Queen Cleapatra

Queen Cleapatra

Eight weeks old.
Stole my heart.
Language defined.
One kiss can ease the mind.
Hours of walks.
Sun, showers, snow, and all.
Unconditional love.
Meals shared.
Loving stare.
Playful nature eternally unmatched.
Non-human daughter.
Deepest of bonds.
Provide guidance through life's fog.
Best of friends.
Queen, my dog.

16. Texas Toast

Terrific
Elegant
X-factor
Adventurous
Sagacious

Talented
Omnipotent
Altruistic
Succulent
Tenacious

XO Amica Mea XO

17. Artificial Beauty

A life of beauty, simple, true.
In quiet moments, skies of blue.
With every step, a joy to find.
Peace and love in heart and mind.
Through gentle winds and shining light.
We live our days, both soft and bright.
In little things, we see the whole.
A beautiful life, a blessed soul.

18. Freedom of Thinking

Universal manipulation.
Rearrangement of the constellations.

Ideologies to manifest.
Empowerment honored like a crest.

Propelling enlightenment with open sails.
Greatest achievement is to gain wisdom from our fails.

Self-actualization is our targeted goal.
Achievement is not cheap, nor should we sell our soul.

Glory is peace, by dismissal of opinions.
I serve the magnificence of energetic forces.
By the destruction to incarceration of demonic minions.

19. The Man

A father's love is fierce and true.
With hands of wisdom, he guides you through.
Heart of a lion, a warrior spirit shinning bright.
He is present to comfort, day or night.
With sharp kindness in each word he speaks.
Strength that levitates when your soul is weak.
A silent hero, patient and strong.
A true father's lessons and love will carry you along.

20. The Woman

A mother's love, so pure and deep.
She holds your heart, helps with peaceful sleep.
The tender care, enlightens the way.
And transforms chaos bright as day.
Her gentle touch, her soothing voice.
In her arms, your spirit will rejoice.
The timeless love, always held near.
Memories of a mother will forever be dear.